The Little Book of
THE
GRAND CANYON

By Zack Bush and Laurie Friedman
Illustrated by Vitor Lopes

DEDICATED TO YOU -
OUR WONDERFUL READER

THIS BOOK BELONGS TO:

The **GRAND CANYON** is one of the most amazing sites—not only in the United States but in the entire world.

There's so much to know about this huge, colorful canyon located in Arizona.
Ready to learn more? Just turn the page!

Formation of the **GRAND CANYON** began millions of years ago through a process called erosion.

Erosion is when water, wind, and other natural forces cause rocks and earth to wear away and move to new places. This movement changes the shape of the land.

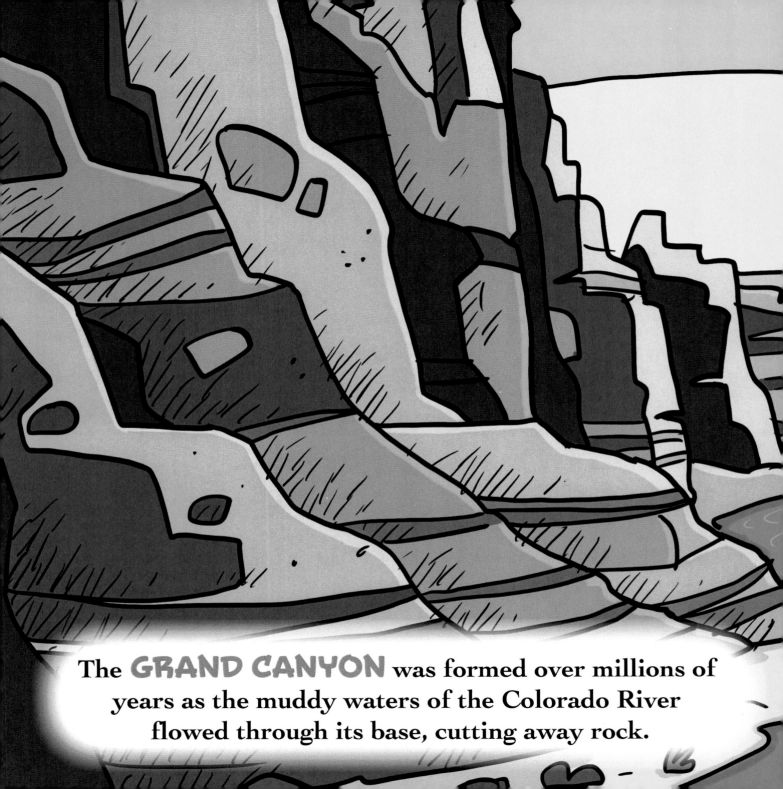

The **GRAND CANYON** was formed over millions of years as the muddy waters of the Colorado River flowed through its base, cutting away rock.

GRAND CANYON NATIONAL PARK was created in 1919.

Millions of tourists visit it every year, making it one of the most visited tourist spots in the world!

The **GRAND CANYON** is 277 miles long, up to 18 miles wide, and over a mile deep.

Some of the rocks in the **GRAND CANYON** are four billion years old!

The layers of rocks, which are called strata, are many beautiful colors, including reds, oranges, pinks, browns, greens, and greys.

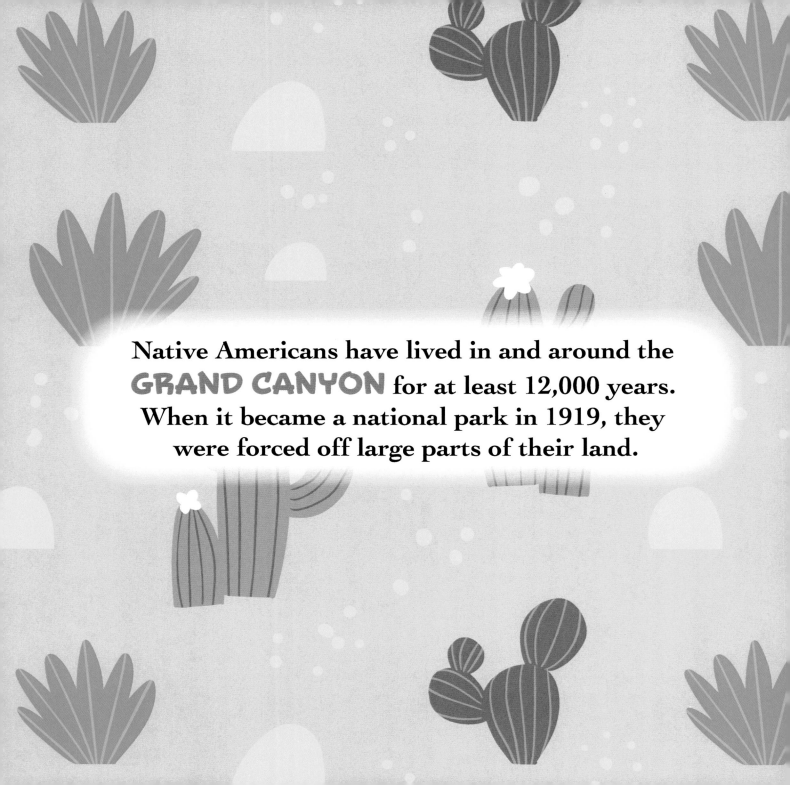

Native Americans have lived in and around the **GRAND CANYON** for at least 12,000 years. When it became a national park in 1919, they were forced off large parts of their land.

Today, there are still some Native American tribes that live and work near the **GRAND CANYON**.

Some members of the tribes work as guides for tourists who come to hike the canyon trails, ride mules along the ridges, and climb the steep rocks.

There are also park rangers who work at **GRAND CANYON NATIONAL PARK**. They are there to help visitors learn about the canyon and to have fun.

Whether you visit the **GRAND CANYON**, read about it from home, or study it at school, there are so many interesting things you can learn.

There are approximately two hundred types of plants and trees in the GRAND CANYON, including willow, fir, spruce, cottonwood, and aspen trees. There are also many types of wildflowers, shrubs, and cacti.

WILLOW

FIR

SPRUCE

COTTONWOOD

ASPEN

WILDFLOWERS

SHRUBS

CACTI

Lots of animals live in the **GRAND CANYON**, including deer, bison, squirrels, foxes, bobcats, rabbits, chipmunks, coyotes, and birds and fish too.

DEER

BISON

SQUIRREL

FOX

BOBCAT

RABBIT

CHIPMUNK

COYOTE

RAVEN

TROUT

The weather in the **GRAND CANYON** is hot in the summer and cold in the winter. It is usually dry because it is located in the desert.

And if you are planning to spend the night, take a jacket. The temperature drops after sundown!

If you visit the **GRAND CANYON**, there are so many fun ways to experience it.

You can bike around the rim of the canyon.

Or take a hike down into the canyon.

You can also take a train ride around the canyon.

One of the coolest ways to see the **GRAND CANYON** is by mule.

The mules take riders to the bottom of the canyon, where they camp out for the night.

If you go to the **GRAND CANYON**, you can go white-water rafting.

You can also see magnificent waterfalls or visit a museum to learn more about the **GRAND CANYON** and its history.

You can even become a Junior Ranger so you can teach others about one of the most special sites in the whole world.

CONGRATULATIONS!
Now you know so much about the GRAND CANYON.

Here's your **GRAND CANYON** badge.
Go ahead. Print it out, pin it on, and maybe one day you will get to visit this special landmark.

Go to the website www.BooksByZackAndLaurie.com
and print out your badges from the
Printables & Activities page.

And if you like this book, please go to
Amazon and leave a kind review.

Keep reading all of the books in #thelittlebookof
series to learn new things and earn more badges.
Other books in the series include:

VALUES/EMOTIONS	ACTIVITIES/IDEAS
The Little Book of Kindness	The Little Book of Camping
The Little Book of Patience	The Little Book of Sports
The Little Book of Confidence	The Little Book of Music
The Little Book of Positivity	The Little Book of Government
The Little Book of Love	The Little Book of Transportation
The Little Book of Good Deeds	The Little Book of Presidential Elections
The Little Book of Responsibility	The Little Book of Grandparents
The Little Book of Curiosity	The Little Book of Bedtime
The Little Book of Gratitude	The Little Book of Good Manners
The Little Book of Friendship	The Little Book of Dance
The Little Book of Laughter	The Little Book of Yoga
The Little Book of Creativity	The Little Book of Healthy Habits
The Little Book of Honesty	The Little Book of Setting Goals
The Little Book of Imagination	The Little Book of Organization
The Little Book of Happiness	The Little Book of Teamwork
The Little Book of Sharing	The Little Book of Baking
The Little Book of Listening	The Little Book of Cooking
The Little Book of Hope	The Little Book of Mindfulness
The Little Book of Cooperation	The Little Book of Adventure

SCIENCE/NATURE

The Little Book of Nature
The Little Book of Outer Space
The Little Book of Going Green
The Little Book of Weather
The Little Book of Pets
The Little Book of Dinosaurs
The Little Book of Plants

MILESTONES/HOLIDAYS

The Little Book of Kindergarten
The Little Book of First Grade
The Little Book of Valentine's Day
The Little Book of Father's Day
The Little Book of Halloween
The Little Book of Giving (Holiday Edition)
The Little Book of Santa Claus
The Little Book of Back to School

LANDMARKS/DESTINATIONS

The Little Book of the Supreme Court
The Little Book of the Grand Canyon

Made in the USA
Coppell, TX
14 May 2024

32386367R00026